THE SUSTAINABLE MODULAR KITCHEN BLUEPRINT

A *Professional Guide* for *Modern-Day Architects* & *New-Age Builders*

THE SUSTAINABLE MODULAR KITCHEN BLUEPRINT

A *Professional Guide* for *Modern-Day Architects* & *New-Age Builders*

Nitin Mehandia

#1 Sustainable Modular Furniture Blueprint

Available on amazonkindle

Worldwide Published by

Pendown Press
PREMIUM BUSINESS PUBLISHER

PENDOWN PRESS LLP

An ISO 9001 & ISO 14001 Certified Co.,

Regd. Office: 3767A, Kanhaiya Nagar,
Tri Nagar, Delhi-110035

Ph.: 8130886000, 9650072927, 8595249536

E-mail: info@pendownpress.com

Branch Office: 1A/2A, 20, Hari Sadan, Ansari Road,
Daryaganj, New Delhi-110002

Ph.: 011-45794768

Website: PendownPress.com

Edition: 2025

Price: ₹ 399

ISBN: 978-93-7217-197-6

Layout and Cover Designed by Pendown Graphics Team

Printed and Bound in India by Thomson Press India Ltd.

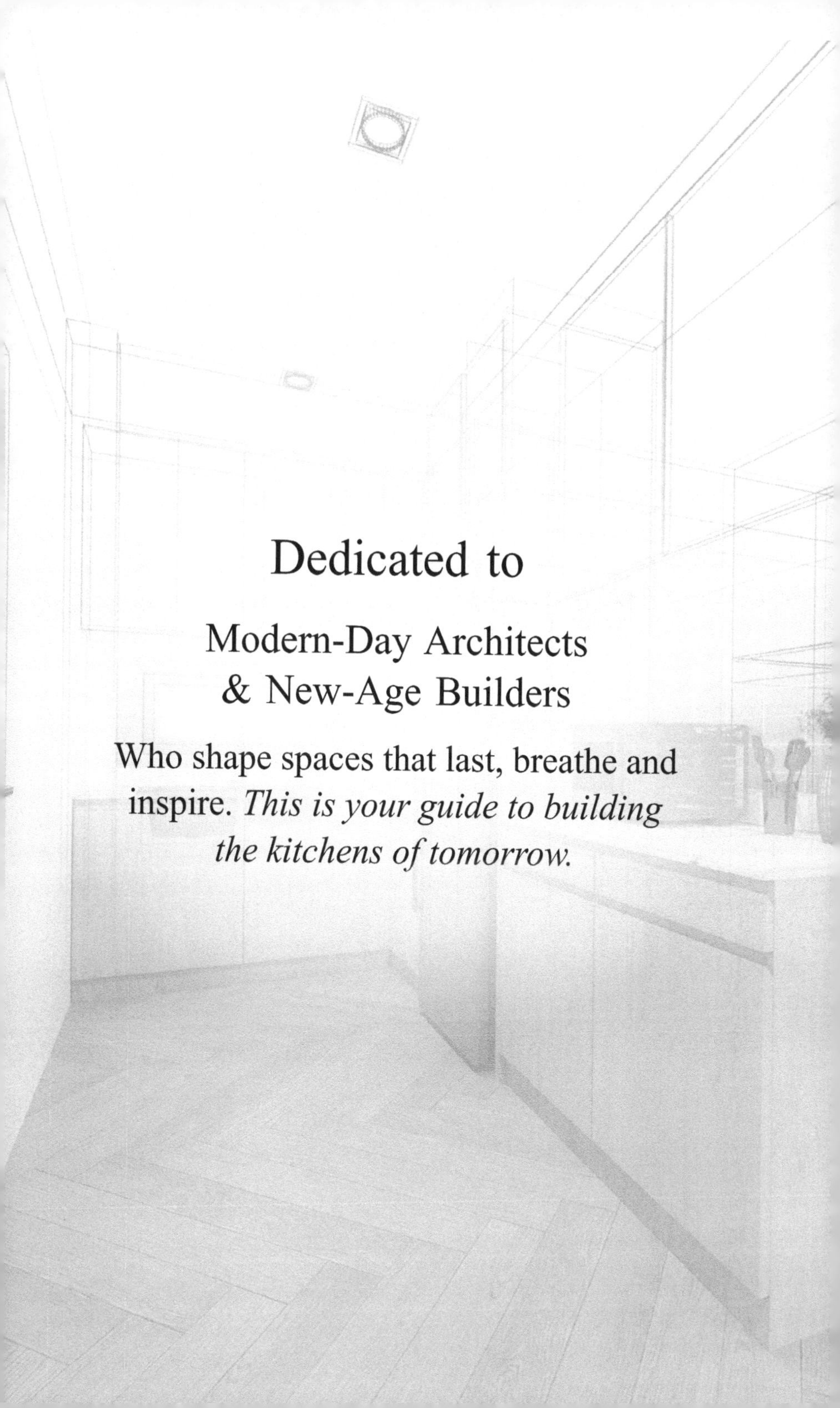

Dedicated to

Modern-Day Architects & New-Age Builders

Who shape spaces that last, breathe and inspire. *This is your guide to building the kitchens of tomorrow.*

Table of Contents

Preface

This book is not written to impress. It is written to help.

Over the years, I've met countless families, homeowners, builders and even young professionals who felt confused or overwhelmed when it came to modular furniture. So many questions, too many choices and very few honest answers. I was one of them once.

This book comes from that space from real experience, real struggles and a real desire to make things simpler for people like you and me.

I've tried to keep everything straightforward, no heavy words, no technical overload. Just clarity, honesty and the kind of knowledge that should've been shared a long time ago.

And if you ever feel stuck while reading, just take a pause. Think of this book not as a rulebook, but like a friend who's walked the path and is now sharing what worked and what didn't, with no hidden agenda.

If even one page helps you avoid a costly mistake or feel more confident about your next step, then this effort is worth it.

Thank you for picking up this book. I truly hope it makes a difference in your journey.

With gratitude,

Nitin Mehandia
#1 Sustainable Modular Furniture Blueprint

Acknowledgments

If I've flown high, it's only because my parents gave me wings. Their love has been my anchor and their faith, my fuel. I've grown because they let me, guided me and believed in me before I believed in myself. They are my lifelong mentors who showed me the path of honesty, transparency and helping others.

My father is deeply committed to sustainability and I learn so much from him about sustainable practices.

To my wife, Preeti Gupta, who has stood by me in every situation. You have handled all family responsibilities, as well as the business journey with great skill and dedication. Thank you from the bottom of my heart.

To my elder sister Renu and elder brother Vipin and to my dearest friends, your unwavering love and presence have been the quiet strength behind every step I've taken. You've stood by me not just in moments of triumph, but through every challenge, as the unshakable pillars of my life's journey.

To my daughters, Asmi and Aadya, who are the source of my happiness and inspiration. Lots of love!

My heartfelt gratitude to all my mentors, Padma Shri Milind Kamble Sir, Padma Shri Ravi Kumar Narra Sir, Sanjiv Dangi Sir, Akshar Yadav Sir, Deepak Pawar Sir and Chetan Jain Sir, who have guided me in my business journey and shown me light and direction.

Special thanks to Mr. Sumit Khubchandani (Director at Jack Martin), Mr. Aman Jain (Director at Dress Man), Mr. R. K. Gupta (Director at RK Marble), Mr. Abhey Goyal (Director at Ajanta Soya Ltd.), Mr. Garvit Arora (Director at Creations), Mr. Raunak Parashar (Director at DIPOLE), Mr. Sunny Pruthi (Director at Alpina Bathroom Products), Mr. Gaurav Pasi (Director at Idea Molecule), Mr. Ankit Khosla (Director at Regal Enterprises), Mr. Avinash Kanodia (Director at Ribbel International Ltd.), and Mr. Prateek Jaiswal (Director at Qaaleen) for inspiring me to write this book.

To my team, your commitment, creativity and constant support have played a huge role in making this dream come true. You are the backbone of everything we do and I feel proud to have you by my side. A special thanks to Tamanna for working so hard to help me write this book and to Mohit for providing the most relevant information I needed throughout the process.

To our clients, who have shared their experiences and knowledge with us during this journey, thank you for trusting us and being our inspiration.

A special acknowledgement goes to Dinesh Verma and his exceptional team at Pendown Press. From the initial concept to the final manuscript, their support and expertise have made this book possible.

And finally, to all my loved ones who have been with me on this journey, thank you for your unwavering support, encouragement and affection. Even if your names are not mentioned, you always hold a special place in my heart.

Without the support of all of you, it would not have been possible for me to move forward with confidence.

Author's Corner

From Engineering Curiosity to Industry Leadership: My Path into Modular Furniture Manufacturing

I specialized in Product Design and Manufacturing at Indo Danish College, where I developed a deep interest in precision and quality. From those early days, I was fascinated by how thoughtful design and process can create lasting impact. Upon completing my studies, I was placed at Minda Industries in the Vendor Development Department. My role was to support Tier 2 and Tier 3 suppliers, ensuring they met the high-quality standards required by OEM giants like Toyota, Honda and Suzuki.

Working in the automotive industry taught me a vital lesson: **Quality processes lead to quality products.** I was responsible for implementing stringent production standards at supplier factories, guaranteeing the right product was delivered on time, with zero compromises. This experience instilled in me the importance of **systems thinking, precision in execution and the power of continuous improvement.**

However, my entrepreneurial drive led me to a new path. Facing financial constraints, I started with labor contracts in 2010, managing brickwork, plastering, false ceilings and interior works for projects like Sharda University, Ahluwalia Contracts and GMR Terminal 3. These were foundational years where I learned to manage complexity, people and expectations all under tight deadlines. By 2012, we expanded into handling material orders. By 2013, we had grown further, taking on full-fledged design-and-build projects and successfully completing over 5 lakh sq ft of built spaces.

But it was during these large-scale projects that I started noticing recurring challenges in modular furniture execution, misaligned panels, sizing issues and coordination gaps between teams. Unlike the automotive industry, where every product undergoes multiple revisions before mass production, modular furniture projects often require rapid execution, sometimes within just 15-30 days. There was no room for error, yet the systems in place were not built for precision or consistency.

I saw this challenge as an opportunity to innovate. **Believing that the more complex an industry, the greater the chance to excel, I founded our modular furniture factory in November 2015.** It wasn't just a business; it was a mission to bring structure, scalability and sustainability into this space. However, we quickly identified inefficiencies, especially in managing flat-pack panels. To address this, I studied the best practices of the world's leading modular furniture factories and integrated their approaches into our operations.

Today, as we produce high-quality modular furniture, **my focus remains the same: precision, process optimization and delivering excellence**. Our clients, builders, architects and end customers demand seamless execution and we meet this challenge through structured processes, cutting-edge machinery and an unwavering commitment to quality.

This journey from product design to modular furniture manufacturing has been driven by one core belief:

True sustainability comes from solving real-world problems with long-term thinking.

My vision is to design and build kitchens that are thoughtfully crafted to last for years, with minimal environmental impact.

> ***"Yeh safar ek engineer ki curiosity se Shuru hua tha, aur aaj ek industry benchmark ban gaya hai."***

Why This Book Matters?

This book is your complete guide to building a sustainable modular kitchen that lasts 20+ years. Sustainability, in our view, isn't limited to using eco-friendly or certified materials. It's about how a kitchen is designed, constructed and assembled to ensure fewer quality issues, minimal replacements and consistently high performance. A kitchen should look beautiful, function smoothly and stay strong for years- without becoming a source of frustration over time.

We believe in practical sustainability where materials are not only environmentally conscious but also selected for their real-world usability, strength and relevance to Indian homes. Even commonly available materials like particle boards can be incredibly durable when integrated with precision and process.

That's why this book goes beyond materials. It dives deep into the actual process because no matter how premium the raw material, a flawed execution can shorten the kitchen's life. We share globally accepted best practices and proven construction techniques that improve longevity and reduce service issues over time.

At the heart of this book is a powerful philosophy:

Sustainable kitchens are born from sustainable thinking.

Every design, decision and detail should come from a mindset rooted in long-term value, efficiency and responsibility.

Through this book, we share not just *what* to build, but *how* to think, *what* to avoid and *how* to get it right the first time. Whether you're a homeowner, architect, or interior designer, this book will give you the confidence and clarity to create kitchens that are durable, beautiful and responsibly made.

Who This Book Is For?

This book is for:

- **Interior Designers:** If you're designing modern homes and want kitchens that are not just good-looking but functionally superior, this book gives you clarity and confidence in your specifications.
- **Builders & Developers:** For those who want their flats or villas to stand out with long-lasting, low-maintenance kitchens. Learn how modular solutions can reduce complaints and boost buyer satisfaction.
- **Modular Kitchen Dealers & Professionals:** Whether you sell or install, this book deepens your product knowledge from materials to hinges so you can confidently answer client queries and avoid costly mistakes.
- **Homeowners Planning a New Kitchen:** If you're building or renovating your dream kitchen and don't want to rely blindly on vendors, this guide helps you make informed, budget-smart and durable choices.

Your smarter kitchen story begins now. Let's open the first chapter together.

Chapter 1

Why is the Kitchen Such an Important Part of the Home?

The Kitchen is truly the **heart of the home** and its importance goes far beyond just being a place to prepare meals. It's a space where family members gather, where daily routines are anchored and often, where the most meaningful conversations happen. In many homes, it becomes the **center of connection, comfort and care**. Functionally and emotionally, the kitchen is the backbone of household life.

If you think about it, many other parts of the house can endure temporary issues, but the kitchen is a critical zone where its failure impacts the entire home. If the toilet stops working, there are often multiple bathrooms available as alternatives. The bedroom can be adjusted by either sharing rooms or temporarily using a living space as a substitute. However, when the kitchen is out of service, **there is no easy alternative**. The entire family's daily routine is disrupted, whether it's cooking, cleaning, or storing food, making it a non-negotiable part of the house.

A malfunctioning kitchen doesn't just affect meals; it can throw off the schedule, flow and comfort of everyone in the house. Without a functioning kitchen, you lose the ability to prepare food, which is essential for both health and emotional well-being. Whether it's cooking a family dinner, preparing snacks, or simply storing essentials, the kitchen serves as the foundation for all these day-to-day activities.

Because of this, the kitchen should always be given the utmost attention when designing or renovating a home. The materials, layout and overall functionality of the kitchen are crucial. A durable, effective and functional kitchen ensures that the household can continue to operate smoothly even during the most demanding times. It isn't just about longevity; it's about designing a space that supports the people who live in it.

Investing in a well-designed kitchen means ensuring that the house's heart is strong and reliable, making it a true centerpiece of the home. From storage solutions to durability, from safety to aesthetics, everything about the kitchen should reflect its importance. It's not just about cooking, it's about creating a space that enhances the overall quality of life in the home. That's why it's important to make sure the kitchen is top-notch in every way: functional, efficient and built to last. After all, when everything else is in order but the kitchen isn't working, everything else can feel like it's falling apart.

So, let's make sure the kitchen remains the essential, dependable space that keeps the home running seamlessly not just today, but for many years to come.

Why Builders & Designers Can't Afford to Treat the Kitchen as "Just Another Room"

The kitchen isn't just another part of a home; it's often the **defining feature** in a buyer's mind. Overlooking it is no longer an option for serious builders or design professionals. Here's why:

1. **Market Impact: The Kitchen Sells the Home**

   80 % of buyers rank the kitchen among their top-three decision factors. If it disappoints, the deal dies before the tour even reaches bedroom #1. *ramseysolutions.com*

   A **Zillow analysis** of 2019-20 listings found that homes advertising premium kitchen features (steam ovens, smart appliances, quartz countertops) fetched **3-5 % price premiums** over their estimate. *zillow.com*

   A great kitchen doesn't just help sell the home; it helps sell it faster and for more.

2. **Price Premium & ROI**

   A thoughtful kitchen upgrade typically recoups **75-81 % of its cost** at resale making it one of the highest ROIs in residential construction. *ramseysolutions.com*

   Remodel economists still lean on the **"5-15 % rule"**: spend (and expect to gain) roughly that slice of total home value when the kitchen is executed well. *zillow.com*

   It's not just an upgrade. It's an investment.

3. **Demand Is Moving to Modular (Especially in India)**

   India's modular-kitchen market hit **USD 4.5 B in 2024** and is racing toward a **24% CAGR through 2031.** This clearly signals that today's buyers *expect* factory-finished precision, not site-carpentered guesswork. *linkedin.com*

Precision and pre-fabrication are the future especially in urban India.

4. **Lifetime Value vs. Planned Obsolescence**

   A well-engineered kitchen lasts **10+ years** before needing major renovations.

   kitchenrenovationmarkham.ca

   - Poor layout, cheap hardware, or sloppy tolerances slash that in half, forcing owners back into dust and demolition within a decade.

   Long-term value comes only from doing it right the first time.

5. **What Happens When You Ignore It (Real-World Pain Points)**

Risk	Impact on Builder / Designer	Supporting Insight
Aesthetic Mis-Match	Disjointed kitchen lowers perceived home quality	Luxury brokers note a *"dated or sad kitchen kills the deal in 10 steps." mansionglobal. com*
Price Erosion	Buyers walk away or negotiate hard if a kitchen upgrade is pending	Same source reports luxury homes sitting unsold purely due to the kitchen.

Reputation Hits	Post-handover complaints stick to the designer's name long after site hand-over	Negative buyer feedback clusters around daily-use pain points.
Costly Call-Backs	Re-work & warranty claims can wipe out margins	Each misaligned hinge or poorly cut panel means on-site delays and loss.

The cost of cutting corners shows up long after handover and it sticks to your name.

6. **The Payoff of Getting It Right**

   Speed: Updated kitchens shorten days-on-market (agents routinely cite faster closes when the kitchen "wows"). **zillow.com**

   - **Durability:** Micro-level CAD that locks in screw positions and drilling depths keeps tolerances under **0.1 mm**, significantly reducing installation errors.
   - **Sustainability:** Precision manufacturing minimizes waste, improves material yield and supports **energy-efficient appliance** integration, key demands for today's environmentally conscious buyers.

> ***"Ghar toh deewar aur chhat se banta hai, lekin kitchen hi hota hai jahan se ghar mein zindagi chalti hai aur agar us jagah mein sukoon na ho, toh poora ghar adhoora lagta hai."***

Chapter 2

Engineering Behind Designing Precision Through Automation

The Role of Software in Achieving Precision

Creating a high-quality modular kitchen requires more than just great visuals; it demands **technical precision**. Most general CAD software used for kitchen design focuses on 2D elevations and 3D views. While helpful for client presentations, these tools fall short when it comes to actual production needs.

The problem? These tools **don't define drilling points, joinery details, or exact hardware positioning**. As a result, what looks good on-screen often breaks down during execution leading to misalignment, inconsistent finishes and costly rework on-site.

This is where **engineering-grade CAD software** comes into play.

Unlike basic design tools, these advanced platforms allow for **micro-level planning.** Every screw, hinge and fitting is precisely mapped and digitally positioned, ensuring that the final product is not just beautiful, but also production-ready.

Key Capabilities of Engineering CAD Tools

- **Precise drilling and joinery details:** Define every screw hole, dowel joint and fastener position with engineering-grade accuracy.
- **Accurate hardware positioning:** Ensure perfect placement for hinges, handles, channels and lift-ups eliminating trial and error.
- **Flawless component alignment:** Achieve tight tolerances and gap-free construction across shutters, carcasses and panels.
- **Material and cut-list optimization:** Automate board planning and reduce waste with intelligent nesting and sizing.
- **Collision/interference checks:** Detect and resolve design conflicts before a single board is cut.

By eliminating manual guesswork, these tools ensure a seamless transition from design to execution resulting in durable, consistent and high-performing kitchens.

The Real Game Changer:
Proper Software Implementation

Having advanced software is just the start. The true impact lies in how it's implemented. Think of Excel: one person uses it for simple lists, while another builds dynamic dashboards. The same applies to design tools; **the outcome depends on how intelligently the system is used.**

When it comes to engineering-grade CAD tools like IMOS, 20-20, CADT, PYTHA, etc., success depends on **intelligent**

integration into your workflow. Without a structured approach, even the best software remains underutilized.

To unlock its full potential, the software must work in sync with:

- **Parametric design logic**
- **Machine-compatible outputs**
- **Production process alignment**

What Engineering-Grade Software Controls

These tools go beyond surface-level visuals they take charge of critical micro-level elements such as:

- **Screw Placement:** Optimized for strength and accuracy
- **Hinge Type & Position:** Predefined for flawless fit
- **Leg Locations:** Auto-calculated for balance and load
- **Drilling Maps:** CNC-ready with perfect alignment
- **Hardware Compatibility:** System-driven selections
- **Material Detailing:** Accurate thickness, finish and grain direction

Benefits of Engineering-Driven Design

- Ultra-low error margin (≤ 0.1 mm tolerance)
- Faster manufacturing and assembly cycles
- Longer product lifespan with reduces wear and tear
- Consistent quality, batch after batch
- Superior finish and fit
- Fewer customer complaints

Conclusion: From Concept to Completion, Engineered to Perform

High-quality furniture isn't a result of guesswork, it's the result of **engineering-backed design**.

With intelligent systems like IMOS, every drawer, shutter and panel is digitally mapped before a single cut is made. This ensures precision at every step, **reducing errors, saving time and elevating quality.**

This is **engineered craftsmanship**:

Where digital accuracy meets skilled execution to create kitchens that are **visually stunning, functionally flawless and built to last.**

> ***"Jab design ho software se linked,***
> ***toh har drawer slide kare synced."***

Chapter 3

Barcode Stickers: Simplifying Installation & Communication

In modular furniture manufacturing, speed and accuracy are non-negotiable especially during large-scale production and on-site installation. One of the simplest yet most effective tools to streamline the entire process is the use of **barcode stickers,** which assign every panel a **unique digital identity**.

Every Panel = Its Own Aadhaar Card

Just like every citizen in India has a unique Aadhaar number, **each furniture component** can be tagged with a **unique barcode ID**. This ID can contain essential information such as:

- Panel dimensions and material
- Part name (e.g., top panel, side panel)
- Job or project reference
- Drilling instructions or fitting type
- Final installation location

This barcode is not just for inventory; it's an integral part of the production and installation workflow.

How Barcode Stickers Help On-Site

As soon as a panel is unboxed at the site, the installer can easily scan or read the barcode sticker to instantly understand:

- Where the panel belongs in the unit
- How it should be oriented and fixed
- What hardware is needed
- Whether any special treatment or handling is required

This reduces dependency on verbal instructions or manual cross-checking. Even **first-time or freelance installers** can confidently and correctly assemble units, **minimizing errors, confusion and delays**.

Conclusion: Smart ID for Smart Furniture

Think of it as your furniture's **Aadhaar system intelligent** tagging that ensures every panel is uniquely identified. It boosts accuracy, speeds up installation and streamlines communication, while adding traceability and accountability to modern modular furniture manufacturing.

In the world of modern modular furniture, barcode stickers are a small detail with massive impact, bridging the gap between factory precision and site-level clarity.

> ***"Panel mile toh sawal nahi, barcode padho, jawab wahi."***

Chapter 4

CNC Drilling: Unmatched Precision & Seamless Installation

In today's modular-furniture ecosystem, **precision is non-negotiable** and **Computer Numerical Control (CNC) drilling technology** is how top manufacturers consistently achieve it.

Critical operations, hinge cups, channel grooves, lock cut-outs, handle placements are routed through design software straight to CNC machines, ensuring each panel is drilled to exact dimensional and positional tolerances that manual methods simply can't replicate.

Why Manual Drilling Falls Short

- **Drawer-channel alignment:** Even the steadiest carpenter introduces subtle angle or position errors when repeating holes across multiple panels.
- **Time cost:** Drilling and aligning a single handle by hand can burn 15–20 minutes on measuring tape, level and pencil marks.
- **Repeatability:** Human fatigue and tiny measurement drift make large-batch consistency nearly impossible.

With CNC, that same handle hole is cut in **under five minutes**, perfectly repeatable every time, across every panel.

The Design-to-Execution Ecosystem

While only a few Indian manufacturers currently operate with full **CAD-to-CNC** integration, this end-to-end ecosystem is already setting new benchmarks in modular precision. Here's how it works:

1. **Panel-specific drill paths:** Generated automatically from parametric cabinet libraries based on your design.
2. **Software-synced drawings:** Drill files sent directly to the CNC's control unit, eliminating the need for manual entry or re-keying.
3. **On-site diagrams & hole maps:** Delivered digitally, allowing installers to follow exact coordinates with zero guesswork.
4. **Plug-and-play hardware fitment**: Channels, hinges and handles fit perfectly on the first try, no trial and error, no rework.

Conclusion: Automation That Installs Confidence

CNC drilling isn't just about faster output; it's about engineering confidence into every screw, hole and slot. It ensures that your furniture doesn't just look great, it fits together with engineering-grade consistency, every time.

We believe that with the right combination of software, machines and skilled people, India can set global benchmarks in modular precision.

> ***"Modular ka magic tabhi chalega,***
> ***jab CNC ka button dabega!"***

Chapter 5

100x More Durable Hinges & Zero Alignment Issues

In modular furniture manufacturing, one of the most recurring and overlooked pain points is the gradual loss of hinge alignment over time. Regardless of whether the carcass is made from Particle Board, MDF, HDHMR or PLY, it is common to witness hinge loosening and door misalignment within 1 to 2 years of installation, sometimes even sooner.

This issue often results in service calls, customer dissatisfaction and a general perception that modular furniture is inherently inferior to traditional methods. Many customers often recall the **old-school continuous piano hinges**, the long metal strips with **20–30 screws per hinge**. These older systems had one major advantage:

Even if a few screws loosened, the **remaining ones held the line**, maintaining alignment and strength over decades.

The Engineering Gap in Modern Modular Design

Most modular furniture shutters rely on:

- 2 - 5 concealed hinges per shutter,
- With only 2 screws fixed into the carcass and 2 into the shutter.

This minimal hardware footprint, while sleek and efficient in appearance, creates a single point of failure. If even one screw loosens, it compromises the entire door's alignment and functionality, something no customer wants to deal with post-installation.

What's the Real Root Cause?

Surprisingly, the problem **doesn't lie in the board material or hinge brand**. The real flaw is in the lack of engineering reinforcement at the screw joints.

Think of it like this:

Mounting a calendar directly onto a wall without a wall plug can lead to failure over time, even a fan breeze or minimal vibration can cause it to fall.

In contrast, if you use a PVC wall plug (sleeve), that same wall can support a much heavier object like a TV dish, which can handle high-pressure winds, but you rarely see it come out from the wall. The difference lies in the engineering detail, not the wall itself.

Engineering-Led Solution: Threaded Hinge Sleeves

To address this fundamental flaw, we introduced a specially designed high-durability **Threaded Hinge Sleeve** insert that ensures superior screw retention and long-term performance.

Key Features:

- **Pre-formed internal threading:** Unlike generic sleeves that rely on the screw to create threads, our sleeve ensures a secure grip from the outset.
- **High-load endurance:** Designed specifically for hinges, where the most wear and tear occurs.
- **Precision fit:** Reduces the risk of misalignment due to wear or screw loosening.

Why Not Channel Sleeves?

There is often confusion between hinge sleeves and channel sleeves. While both are anchoring solutions, they serve very different purposes and using them interchangeably can lead to serious long-term issues.

Channel sleeves are commonly used in drawers, locks, legs and runners, but they are not suitable for hinges and here's why:

- Their collar height can cause unwanted sound or vibration when used in high-movement zones.
- They lack the thread precision and load distribution required for hinge applications.
- They tend to wear out after 3–4 rounds of screw tightening, making them unsuitable for long-term structural roles.

In contrast, Threaded Hinge Sleeves are designed for repeat use, high performance and zero alignment failure even under daily stress.

Real-World Consequences of Ignoring This Detail

When hinges or runners are screwed directly into Particle board, MDF or HDHMR without proper reinforcement:

- Screws may loosen over time due to internal material fatigue.
- The screw cap may break off inside the fitting, damaging the inner wall of the channel.
- This leads to structural failure, necessitating costly repairs or replacements.

By applying this simple engineering principle, you can dramatically increase the lifespan of your kitchen hinges, eliminate maintenance issues and maintain aesthetic perfection regardless of the material used.

Conclusion:

Modular furniture durability hinges on small yet crucial engineering details. Threaded Hinge Sleeves solve a key industry pain point, ensuring lasting strength. It's not just better furniture, it's about building trust, longevity and stronger customer relationships through smarter solutions.

> *"Zindagi ke har mod pe, ghar ki har chhoti cheez ka apna ehsaas hota hai aur Mazboot Hinges hi use umar lgate hain."*

Chapter 6

100% Shielded: The Ultimate Protection Against Termites & Dampness

In Indian climate conditions where humidity, damp walls and pest risks are frequent, termite infestation and moisture seepage remain two of the most dangerous threats to the longevity of modular furniture.

Even with water-resistant materials and laminates, a tiny 3–4 mm weak spot in typical modular carcass construction can become a silent entry point for damage.

The Hidden Weak Spot in Modular Carcass Designs

Most modular carcasses insert the back panel into routed grooves in the side panels. This creates an unavoidable **3–4 mm gap** around the panel's edge. While not visible after installation, this gap can allow:

- **Moisture** to seep in from damp walls/floors
- **Termites** to enter undetected
- **Slow internal damage** that often goes unnoticed until it's too late

When all external surfaces are sealed with laminate (mica), PVC, or acrylic, this single internal weakness can undermine the entire protection strategy.

Laminates protect surfaces, but unsealed core edges near walls or floors invite problems from behind the scenes.

How to Effectively Seal the Carcass Interior

To eliminate this risk, manufacturers and DIYers alike can adopt **a two-part solution:**

1. **Use a Protective Gap-Covering Cap**

   Install a custom-designed insert or extrusion that caps the 3–4 mm groove where the back panel sits. This physical barrier should:

   - Fully cover the internal cavity, closing off the gap where pests and moisture typically enter
   - Be moisture-resistant (PVC, ABS, or treated aluminum) for long-term protection
   - Redirect any potential water seepage *away* from the carcass interior, preventing internal soaking or swelling

2. **Apply Industrial-Grade Silicone Sealant**

   Once the cavity is capped, apply a continuous bead of antifungal, waterproof silicone around the entire perimeter of the back panel.

   For best results:

   - Use silicone sealants **commonly used in bathrooms or kitchens,** these are engineered for **long-term adhesion in high-humidity zones.**

- Ensure the sealant is **applied smoothly and allowed to cure fully** before installation
- Prefer sealants with **anti-fungal and mold-resistant properties** for added durability

The Importance of Material Selection in Termite-Prone Areas (2017 Case study)

In 2017, a homeowner undergoing a full renovation ahead of a family wedding made an interesting split decision: wardrobes and doors were sourced from a local carpenter, while modular beds, kitchen cabinets and bathroom vanities were purchased from a manufacturer specializing in pre-finished units with engineered protection.

Fast forward a few years and the results offered a clear comparison.

➢ The **locally fabricated elements** including wardrobes, doors and even wooden flooring were severely affected by termite infestation. In some places, termite dust had built up to nearly **6 inches behind the bed's backrest**.

➢ In contrast, the **modular elements**, beds, cabinets and vanities remained completely unaffected, showing **no termite damage or moisture ingress**, despite being in the same environment.

This case highlights the **critical role of manufacturing processes, material selection and pre-treatment methods** in ensuring long-term durability, especially in climates where termite activity and humidity are prevalent. While aesthetics and customization are important, real-world performance often depends on the **technical specifications that lie beneath the surface**.

Additional Benefits of Using a Shielded Carcass System

- **No Need to Tile Behind Cabinets:** A properly sealed carcass system can be installed directly against walls, even damp-prone ones, eliminating the need for costly tiling or cladding behind the units. This results in both material and labor savings.
- **Faster Site Completion:** With factory-level sealing or pre-applied barrier systems, there's no dependency on third-party waterproofing or sealing at the site. This accelerates installation and helps shorten project timelines.
- **Improved Long-Term Durability:** A sealed system helps prevent internal decay from moisture seepage, preserving the structural strength of the furniture over time, especially in humid or high-risk areas.
- **Cost Savings & Peace of Mind:** By pro-actively blocking termite entry points and sealing off moisture paths, you can avoid expensive repairs or replacements down the line. This adds long-term value and reduces after-sales service calls offering greater peace of mind to both manufacturers and homeowners.

Conclusion

While aesthetics often steals the spotlight, **true durability lies beneath the surface**. A well-designed shielded system combining mechanical sealing, smart material selection and precision detailing can drastically improve the lifespan of modular carcasses.

By closing even the tiniest gaps, such systems help defend against moisture seepage and termite intrusion, two of the most common causes of hidden damage. This isn't just surface-level protection, it's a long-term durability strategy, engineered for Indian environments and built to withstand time, use and pests alike.

> ***"Chhup Chhup ke aane waale Dushmanon ke liye, humne banayi ek Anokhi Deewar.***

Chapter 7

Bonded to Perfection - Double Strength Glue + CNC Precision for Ultra-Luxury Panels

---

In modular furniture, aesthetics aren't just a preference, they're a **necessity**. And one of the most critical contributors to that flawless, premium look is **edge banding**. Whether it's a wardrobe, a kitchen shutter, or a storage unit, **cleanly sealed edges** mark the difference between a polished, high-end product and something that feels unfinished.

Why Edge Banding Matters

Edge banding refers to the process of covering the exposed edges of engineered panels (like MDF or particle board) to:

- Create a smooth, professional finish
- Prevent moisture entry
- Enhance resistance to impact and chipping
- Improve the overall lifespan and durability of the furniture

Even a 1 mm misalignment here can ruin the visual appeal, especially in gloss, acrylic, or high-reflection finishes.

Traditionally, this task is handled with **manual or semi-automatic machines**. These machines, while common, can struggle with **precision**, especially when mass-producing furniture with tight quality requirements.

Precision Through High-End Edge Banding Machines

For high-end modular applications, **CNC-operated edge banding machines** offer a significant upgrade. These advanced systems feature:

- **Automated multi-glue compatibility**, including PUR (Polyurethane Reactive) adhesives
- **Consistent application** with minimal manual input
- **Flawless trimming, alignment and corner rounding**, all done at high speed and with repeat accuracy

This level of automation not only ensures **visual consistency**, but also reduces human error making it ideal for luxury-grade finishes where precision is non-negotiable.

The Hidden Hero: Glue Quality

While machine precision is vital, **adhesive quality** is just as critical to long-term performance. Lower-cost adhesives (₹300–₹400/kg) may seem budget-friendly upfront, but often fall short in terms of:

- Bonding strength
- Heat resistance
- Moisture durability

One of the most trusted names in high-performance adhesives is **Kleiberit,** a German-engineered glue known for exceptional bonding and consistency. Though priced at approximately ₹650 - ₹850 /kg, its performance far surpasses regular glues **delivering nearly double the holding strength.**

Bonding Strength Comparison

Adhesive Type	Push Resistance (kg)
Regular adhesives	7–9 kg
Kleiberit or Equivalent Brands	12–13 kg

This additional strength is particularly valuable in areas like kitchens and wardrobes, where **temperature and humidity** fluctuations are common.

Premium Edge Banding Materials

Material quality is the final piece of the edge-banding system and it matters just as much. Industry leaders often turn to **Rehau**, a globally respected brand known for:

- **UV resistance**
- **Thermal stability**
- **Color consistency and durability**

Rehau edge bands are widely used in projects where **aesthetic precision** and **material resilience** are essential. For specialized textures or unique color tones, **E-Square** also offers reliable alternatives with good finish quality.

Conclusion: The Edge that Defines Quality

A superior edge banding result depends on three key elements working together:

1. **CNC precision machinery**
2. **High-performance adhesives**
3. **Premium-quality edge banding tapes**

This strategic combination ensures not only a **visually flawless finish**, but also **long-term durability and resistance** to wear, heat and moisture. For anyone operating in or sourcing from the premium modular furniture segment, **edge banding isn't a minor detail, it's a defining feature of quality.**

> ***"Rehau ki shine, Kleiberit ka spine banaye har panel divine."***

Chapter 8

What to Use & Where to Use?

One of the biggest challenges in modular furniture is knowing **which material is right for which purpose.** There's a flood of information out there blogs, expert opinions, sales pitches and it often leads to more confusion than clarity. The result? We end up with wrong decisions that affect durability, cost, or aesthetics.

That's exactly why this book brings you some crisp comparison between PLY, Particle Board, MDF and HDHMR, so you can understand clearly what to use, where to use it and why.

Water Resistance Comparison: HDHMR vs. Plywood vs. MDF vs. Particle Board

Water resistance is a critical factor in material selection, especially for kitchens, bathrooms and humid environments. Among available options, moisture resistance varies significantly based on material composition, core density and the type of binders used.

1. **HDHMR (High-Density High Moisture Resistance Board) & Equivalent Variants**

   HDHMR is a **generic category name** popularized by **Action Tesa**, but various brands market similar products under different names:

   - **Greenpanel** calls it **HDWR (High-Density Water Resistant Board)**
   - **Crossbond** markets it as **MDHMR (Moisture-Defiant High-Density Board)**
   - Other brands have their own proprietary names for the same category of boards

   Why is HDHMR the best in water resistance?

   - **High density prevents water penetration**, reducing the risk of swelling and warping.
   - Made from **high-quality hardwood fibers**, offering more uniform structure and superior moisture resistance.
   - Uses **Melamine-Urea-Formaldehyde (MUF) and Phenol-Formaldehyde (PF) binders**, both known for enhancing water resistance and dimensional stability.

   HDHMR is widely recommended for under-sink cabinets, bathroom vanities and areas prone to moisture exposure.

2. **Plywood (Marine/BWP Grade) - Highly Water-Resistant**

   - Plywood's water resistance **depends on the type of wood and adhesives used** during manufacturing.
   - **Marine-grade plywood** (BWP - Boiling Water Proof) and **Gurjan core plywood** are known for excellent water resistance.

- Typically bonded with **Phenol-Formaldehyde (PF) resin**, which offers superior waterproofing even under prolonged exposure.

Ideal for wet zones, exterior furniture and heavy-duty applications that demand structural strength with water protection.

3. **MDF (Medium Density Fiberboard) - Moderate Water Resistance**

- **Standard MDF** is **not suitable** for wet environments due to its high-water absorption rate.
- **Exterior grade MDF** is treated with **special binders like MUF and PF resins**, making it more moisture-resistant than regular MDF.
- Best suited for semi-moist conditions but not prolonged water exposure.

Great for design flexibility and smooth finishes, but must be used cautiously in damp conditions.

4. **Particle Board - Generally Weak, but New Variants Offer Better Resistance**

- **Regular particle board** is highly **prone to swelling and internal damage** when exposed to moisture.
- **Exterior-grade particle boards**, such as **Merino's version**, claim to outperform HDHMR in water resistance.
- Typically treated with **MUF or Isocyanate-based binders**, improving its moisture resistance.

Best used for budget applications, but only after verifying actual test reports for water resistance if being considered for moisture-prone zones.

Termite Resistance: Understanding How Different Boards Perform

Termite resistance is a crucial factor when selecting wood-based materials for furniture and interior applications especially in regions prone to pest activity. While **no natural wood is inherently termite-proof,** the level of resistance varies depending on the composition, binders and treatments used in manufacturing.

Why Are Some Boards More Termite - Resistant Than Others?

All engineered boards, **particle board, MDF and HDHMR** are made from **wood fibers or particles bonded with synthetic resins**. These binders play a crucial role in termite resistance. Certain adhesives, like **Melamine-Urea-Formaldehyde (MUF) and Phenol-Formaldehyde (PF) resins**, are **disliked by termites** due to their chemical composition. As a result, termites tend to avoid these materials up to a certain time, making them more resistant compared to solid wood-based plywood.

Case Study: Termite Damage in a Wet Area

At one of our project sites, we observed an interesting scenario:

- A **bathroom door frame** made from **solid wood** was **90% damaged by termites** due to prolonged exposure to moisture.
- Just next to it, **wooden flooring** installed in the same wet conditions remained **completely untouched** by termites.

- The reason? The **binder used in the flooring material** contained chemical compounds that termites found unappealing, effectively deterring infestation.

This case highlights a critical insight: **Termite resistance depends not just on the wood itself but on the resins and binders used in its composition.**

As mentioned earlier, for ultimate protection especially in carcass design, we strongly recommend sealing the back cavity using a back clip or cavity cover, along with anti-fungal silicone for an airtight seal.

Screw-Holding Capacity in Wood-Based Panels

The ability of a material to hold screws depends on its **density, structure and composition**. Here's a comparison of commonly used materials, ranked from highest to lowest screw-holding strength:

1. **HDHMR (High-Density High Moisture Resistant Board)**: **Best screw retention** due to its high density and compact fibers, making it ideal for heavy-duty applications.
2. **Plywood**: **Strong and reliable**, especially when screws are inserted perpendicular to the layers. Edge screwing requires caution to prevent delamination.
3. **MDF (Medium Density Fiberboard)**: **Moderate strength** but prone to splitting if not pre-drilled. Works best with specialized MDF screws.
4. **Particle Board**: **Weakest screw-holding ability** due to its coarse structure.

For **better durability and grip in all boards**, we recommend using **threaded ABS sockets with matching screws**, ensuring secure and long-lasting joints.

Dimensional Accuracy

Dimensional accuracy refers to a material's ability to maintain **consistent thickness, flatness and stability** without warping or expansion. This factor plays a crucial role in ensuring **precise joins, seamless finishes** and **machine compatibility,** especially in modular and CNC-based manufacturing.

Here's how commonly used boards compare:

1. **MDF (Medium Density Fiberboard): Best Accuracy**
   - Made from fine wood fibers bonded with resin under high pressure, MDF has a **uniform density** and **precise thickness**, making it ideal for CNC machining and detailed cuts.
2. **HDHMR (High-Density High Moisture Resistant Board): Best Accuracy**
   - A denser version of MDF, HDHMR offers **excellent stability** with **minimal expansion**, even in moisture-prone environments.
3. **Particle Board: Good Accuracy**
   - Despite being made of compressed wood chips, modern manufacturing techniques ensure **consistent thickness**, making it suitable for precise applications when properly sealed.

4. **Plywood: Moderate Accuracy**
    - Unlike engineered boards, plywood consists of multiple veneer layers and **each layer can have thickness variations.** Sometimes, layers are bonded with slight overlaps, leading to **tolerance issues.**
    - For example, if we plan for **16mm plywood** and apply **0.8mm laminate on both sides**, the expected final thickness should be **17.6mm.** However, due to **plywood's thickness variation (±0.5mm or more)**, the final size can deviate, making **trim lines unmanageable** and impacting overall aesthetics.

Overall Finish

The surface finish of a board plays a vital role in its aesthetic appeal, ease of painting or polishing and how well it can bond with laminates or veneers. A superior finish not only enhances appearance but also reduces preparation time in finishing processes.

Here's how commonly used materials compare:

1. **MDF (Medium Density Fiberboard): Best Finish**
    - Offers a **smooth and uniform surface**, making it perfect for **painting, lacquering and laminating.**
    - With no visible grains or joints, MDF provides a **seamless, flawless finish.**
2. **HDHMR (High-Density High Moisture Resistant Board): High-Quality Finish**
    - Similar to MDF but denser, HDHMR provides **better moisture resistance** while maintaining a smooth, refined surface.

- It accepts **laminates and veneers well**, resulting in an elegant finish suitable for premium applications.

3. **Particle Board: Moderate Finish**

   Particle Board has a **rougher surface** compared to MDF and HDHMR but is suitable for **laminates and melamine coatings**.

   - Direct painting is not recommended due to its porous structure, but it works well with **pre-finished surfaces**.

4. **Plywood: Surface Finish Challenges**
   - While plywood can offer a **natural wood look**, its **surface quality varies**. The **layered structure** of plywood leads to **uneven thickness and undulations**, making it prone to imperfections.
   - These inconsistencies result in a **less smooth finish**, which can impact aesthetics and require additional surface treatment or veneering for a polished look.

Weather Impact on Laminated & Edge-Banded Boards in Modular Furniture

When **laminates are applied on both sides** and **edges are sealed with edge banding**, the performance of all engineered boards improves significantly. These protective layers act like a barrier against moisture and temperature changes, enhancing the material's real-world durability. Here's how different boards behave in real-world Indian weather conditions:

1. **Particle Board: Surprisingly Stable in Indian Weather**
   - **When laminated on both sides and fully edge-banded, Particle Board remains highly stable** in varying temperatures and humidity.
   - It **does not warp, bend, or expand**, making it a cost-effective and reliable choice for modular furniture.
2. **HDHMR: High Moisture Resistance**
   - Even without lamination, HDHMR has **inherent moisture resistance,** thanks to its high-density core and moisture-repellent binders.
   - With **laminate and edge banding, it remains exceptionally stable**, making it a premium choice for areas with prolonged humidity exposure.
3. **MDF: Stable in Controlled Conditions**
   - **Lamination and edge banding prevent direct moisture absorption**, but MDF is still **slightly prone to swelling** if humidity seeps in through screw holes or joints.
   - Performs well in **moderate humidity but is less suited for extreme conditions**.
4. **Plywood: Moderate Stability Due to Layered Structure**
   - Laminated plywood performs well, but due to **natural wood veneer layers**, it can still experience **minor movement (expansion or contraction) in extreme weather**.
   - **BWP-grade plywood is better** for high-moisture areas.

Density Comparison of Wood-Based Boards (kg/m³)

Density plays a crucial role in **strength, screw-holding capacity and durability**. It affects how well a material handles weight, fasteners and long-term use. Here's how different boards compare in terms of density:

1. **HDHMR (High-Density High Moisture Resistant Board): 850-900 kg/m³**
   - Highest density among all engineered boards
   - Offers excellent screw-holding capacity and high-resistance to moisture and impact
2. **MDF (Medium Density Fiberboard): 700-800 kg/m³**
   - Lower density than HDHMR but still strong and stable for most interior applications
   - Smooth, uniform surface ideal for painting and laminates
3. **Plywood: 600-750 kg/m³** *(Varies by grade and composition)*
   - **Less dense than MDF and HDHMR** due to its layered structure
   - Strength depends on wood species and adhesive quality
4. **Particle Board – 550-650 kg/m³**
   - **Lowest density** among all engineered boards
   - Lightweight but weaker in screw-holding and load-bearing, especially without proper reinforcement

Industry Perception vs. Practical Application

In the Indian market, particle boards are often misunderstood and underestimated. While many perceive it as weak or unreliable, this is largely inaccurate when seen globally. Top international and Indian brands like Häcker, Wren, Nolte, Nobilia and other reputed German kitchen manufacturers extensively use 100% particle board in their modular furniture systems. Even their basic 8ft kitchens start at ₹12–15 lakh, proving that this material choice is driven by engineered design, not cost-cutting.

The key to long-lasting performance with particle boards lies in correct engineering and hardware use, especially the use of sleeves or threaded inserts for screw reinforcement, which significantly enhance durability and reduce failure. With proper application, modular kitchens and wardrobes using particle board have consistently lasted over 10 years of daily use without failure.

For wet zones like under the sink, HDHMR is ideal due to its high moisture and termite resistance. However, for dry areas like wardrobes, particle board is superior. For instance, in a 2x8 ft vertical wardrobe shutter, HDHMR's high density can cause sagging over time, whereas a particle board's lighter weight preserves shape and structural integrity.

In kitchen design, the ideal material mix includes:

- **HDHMR** for wet areas (e.g., under-sink cabinets),
- **MDF or particle board** for the remaining carcass and shutters where surface finish, machining precision and weight balance are critical.

Conclusion

There is no single "best" material for all purposes. Every board: Ply, MDF, HDHMR and Particle Board has its pros and cons. The key is to select the right material for the right location, balancing technical properties with design needs and budget.

Material intelligence is not about using the costliest or the strongest materials, but about using the most appropriate one.

Particle board, MDF and HDHMR boards are all green-certified, eco-friendly choices for your sustainable kitchen. Plywood relies on cut timber and chemical glues, so it's not the greenest pick for a sustainable kitchen.

> *"Sahi samajh, sahi choice furniture ki kahani wahi hoti hai jahan har board apni jagah pe hota hai."*

Chapter 9

Pre-Laminated vs Post-Laminated Boards: Understanding the Difference

In the world of modular furniture manufacturing, one of the most critical choices that determines both the visual finish and long-term durability of furniture is the selection between Pre-Laminated and Post-Laminated boards. While both serve the purpose of providing a decorative finish to engineered boards like MDF, Particle Board, or HDHMR, the method of application significantly affects quality, cost and performance.

Understanding this difference is essential not just for manufacturers, but also for architects, designers and homeowners aiming for lasting value. A board may look the same from the outside, but how its laminate is applied can define how it performs over years of use.

Let's break down what truly separates pre-laminated boards from post-laminated ones and how to make the right choice based on application, durability needs and finish expectations.

What is a Pre-Laminated Board?

Pre-Laminated boards are factory-produced panels in which the decorative surface (also referred to as the laminate layer) is already bonded to the board during manufacturing. The process involves:

- Precise glue application
- Heat and pressure bonding under industrial-grade conditions
- Smooth and uniform finish ensured by calibrated machinery

This means the board reaches the furniture manufacturer ready-to-use, with a smooth, pre-applied decorative surface.

Key Advantages:

- **Superior Finish Quality:** Industrial lamination ensures an even, flawless surface without air bubbles or inconsistencies.
- **Lower Cost:** Only a single lamination step is required, saving on labor and materials.
- **Time Efficient:** No additional pasting is needed at the production unit, reducing lead times.
- **Reduced Error Margin:** Controlled factory conditions result in consistent thickness and finish, even in large batches.

What is a Post-Laminated Board?

In Post-Laminated boards, the laminate sheet (commonly known as Sunmica or Mica) is glued onto the raw board manually or using in-house hydraulic or roller presses. This is typically done by pasting the laminate which itself is pre-pasted on a black Bakelite base, onto the base board.

The process includes:

- Manual or semi-automatic glue application
- Pressing using local machines
- Additional curing and handling time

Key Disadvantages:

- **Double Pasting Costs:** The laminate is first pasted on Bakelite during its manufacturing and then again on the board, doubling the glue and increasing material cost.
- **Finish Inconsistency:** Manual glue application often leads to uneven thickness and surface undulations.
- **Longer Production Time:** Additional processing steps delay the workflow.
- **Higher Material Wastage:** Inaccurate pressing and trimming may result in surface defects.

Conclusion: Which One Should You Choose?

For manufacturers prioritizing precision, speed, cost-efficiency and surface quality, **Pre-Laminated boards** clearly emerge as the superior choice. They offer consistent finish, fewer errors and faster production.

While **Post-Laminated boards** may still be useful for certain custom or niche applications, they come with higher risks such as finish variation, longer curing time, increased costs and greater chances of wastage.

In today's quality-conscious and fast-paced furniture market, ***Pre-Lam is the smarter, more future-ready solution.***

> ***"Jab har detail ho perfect, toh kyun karein compromise? Pre-Laminated boards hi best advice!"***

Chapter 10

The Right Hinge, The Right Move: Tiny Detail, Big Impact in Modular Furniture

---

When it comes to modular furniture, even the smallest components can significantly influence functionality and customer satisfaction. One such critical component is the hinge, often overlooked, but essential in delivering a smooth user experience, long-lasting durability and refined aesthetics. Choosing the right hinge can transform a good cabinet into a great one.

Understanding the Hinge Market

In the Indian modular furniture industry, Hettich, Häfele and Ebco are among the most widely recognized and trusted brands. Each offers a variety of hinge types, but not all are created equal, especially when it comes to performance, cost and adjustability.

Hettich Hinges: Onsys vs. Sensys

Hettich offers two primary hinge models:

1. **Onsys Hinge**
    - Budget-friendly
    - Limited adjustability
    - Not recommended for premium modular furniture
    - Known to lack smoothness in motion and finish in long-term use
2. **Sensys Hinge**
    - Premium product with advanced engineering
    - Features smooth soft-close functionality without jerky movements
    - Offers excellent 3-way adjustability: Left, Right and Depth, making installation and alignment much easier
    - Delivers superior aesthetics and a consistent, silent close every time
    - Highly reliable in long-term performance

Our Recommendation: Always prefer Sensys over **Onsys for modular furniture** where quality, durability and end-user experience matter.

Issues with Alternatives: Ebco and Häfele

While Ebco and Häfele also offer soft-close hinges, earlier versions were found to have certain usability issues:

➢ **Soft-close malfunction:** On opening the shutter up to ~30 degrees, it would abruptly snap shut, a counterproductive user experience.

- **Limited adjustability** in traditional hinge models, which made alignment particularly difficult in modern handle-less or flush shutter designs.
- **Inconsistent motion quality,** especially in high-use kitchen zones.

These issues led to frequent on-site adjustments, service calls and ultimately affected customer satisfaction.

Our Recommendation

Based on years of field testing and hands-on application:

- **For premium modular furniture:** Use Hettich Sensys hinges for unmatched quality, adjustability and user comfort.

Conclusion

Hinges may seem like a small part of modular furniture, but they play a big role in functionality, durability and user satisfaction. Choosing the right hinge, especially those with 3D adjustment and reliable soft-close can eliminate customer complaints, enhance product performance and simplify installation. Whether you're building for luxury or value, investing in the right hinge is a small decision that creates a major impact.

Whether you're building a ₹1 lakh kitchen or a ₹5 lakh one, **the right hinge sets the tone** for everything that follows.

> ***"Chhoti si hinge, bada farq, har band darwaza khol deta hai khushi ka raasta!"***

Chapter 11

Key Factors for a Perfect Sink Unit in Indian Kitchens

When designing a modular kitchen, one of the most debated decisions is:

Single-bowl or double-bowl sink?

While both have their place, functionality should drive the decision, especially in Indian homes where heavy-duty cooking, oil-based meals and large utensils are part of daily life.

What Real Homemakers Say

We spoke with 50+ homemakers who actively use their kitchens every day. Surprisingly, **93% preferred a single-bowl sink** over a double-bowl option.

Why the Shift from Double-Bowl to Single-Bowl?

- **Traditional Double-Bowl Sinks:** One bowl typically measures around 450 mm and the other is 300 mm. Sounds versatile, right? But here's what actually happens:
- **Accessory Clash:** Two bowls = No room left for drip trays, soap dispensers, or filter taps. Everything feels cramped.

- **Limited Usability:** Large utensils like kadhais, pressure cookers, tawas, or mixing bowls barely fit. You end up awkwardly tilting or spilling, negating the supposed "advantage" of two bowls.
- **Uneven Use:** Most users admit they only use one bowl. The second bowl becomes a drying zone, waste bin, or simply stays empty.

Why Single-Bowl Sinks Are Winning in Indian Homes

Single-bowl sinks, especially the wider ones (24"-30") are proving far more efficient and clutter-free. Here's why:

- **Spacious Scrubbing Zone:** Easily fits large vessels without stacking or overlap.
- **Better Handling:** Cleaning big, curved or flat cookware becomes simpler and faster.
- **Less Splashing:** Especially when paired with a side-mounted drip tray, water drainage is cleaner and tidier.
- **Simpler Plumbing:** Fewer joints and pipes mean less clogging and easier maintenance.
- **Cleaner Look:** One defined sink space integrates seamlessly with the countertop, especially with quartz or granite.

Final Takeaway

In the Indian kitchen context, form must follow function. While double-bowl sinks offer a certain aesthetic, single-bowl sinks win on practicality, space efficiency and day-to-day usability.

If your clients are daily cooks, prioritize utility over novelty. A well-designed single-bowl setup paired with the right accessories, offers the best blend of ergonomics, hygiene and efficiency.

Sink Tap Placement: Wall-Mounted vs. Sink-Mounted

Another important design decision is the **positioning of the faucet:**

Sink-Mounted Taps:

- Common due to ease of installation, especially when sinks come pre-drilled
- Convenient during factory fabrication or quick fit-outs

Wall-Mounted Taps:

- **Reduced water seepage** into the carcass below the sink
- **More counter space** in front of the sink for day-to-day use
- **Easier maintenance and access** for plumbing repairs

While both options are viable, wall-mounted taps often offer better long-term maintenance and cabinet protection, particularly in moisture-prone zones.

If choosing a sink-mounted tap, ensure the sink is designed for it with appropriate reinforcement and alignment to avoid leaks or installation errors.

Takeaway: Match Form with Function

There's no one-size-fits-all answer, but for most Indian homes, the combination of:

- A **large single-bowl sink** (24-30 inches)
- A **side drip tray for drainage and drying**
- A **wall-mounted tap for better maintenance and hygiene**

A strong balance of **durability, usability** and **long-term performance.**

Designing a great kitchen isn't just about looks, it's about anticipating how the space will perform **years down the line**.

> *"Har paani ki boond, har bartan ki safai,*
> *Kitchen ki khamosh kahani hai ye sink."*

Chapter 12

Precision in Stone Cutting for a Durable Kitchen

When designing a modular kitchen, the spotlight often falls on materials, finishes and brand choices. But in reality, precision stone cutting, especially around the sink unit- can determine whether a kitchen lasts 20 years or starts deteriorating in just 2. Water, if not properly controlled, is the kitchen's silent destroyer.

Top-Mounted vs. Undermount Sinks: What Really Works

While **undermount sinks** are popular for their sleek look, they pose several long-term risks if not installed with absolute precision, something often overlooked in the Indian context.

Common Issues with Undermount Sinks:

- **Challenging Installation:** Most use clip-based systems, which are rarely installed correctly by local fabricators. If even one clip fails or adhesive gaps form, it compromises the entire waterproofing.
- **Circle-Cut Precision:** Cutting a perfect circle in granite or quartz requires advanced machinery often unavailable

on-site. Manual cutters may leave uneven edges, causing water seepage or poor fit.

- **Invisible Gaps, Visible Damage:** Even a micro-gap between stone and sink allows water seepage, damaging the carcass below. The damage becomes noticeable only when it's too late. By the time swelling appears, the board integrity is often already compromised.

For these reasons, **top-mounted (drop-in) sinks** are generally more reliable and installation-friendly, especially in Indian conditions.

How to Install a Top-Mounted Sink the Right Way

Incorrect sink cutouts are a common cause of carcass swelling near the sink unit. A better approach includes:

- **Preserving the stone collar:** Instead of cutting out the entire sink shape, retain the collar edge. This provides better weight support and a firmer sink resting surface. This also helps in avoiding direct water exposure to the core panel edges, especially in daily high-splash areas.
- **Using high-quality silicone sealant:** Seal all edges thoroughly to prevent leaks especially at the back where the faucet sits. Choose anti-fungal, waterproof-grade silicone designed for kitchen or bathroom use to ensure a lasting seal.

Even minor misalignments or poorly sealed joints can lead to **fungal growth, carcass bloating and structural failure** within 2–4 years. Once swelling begins, the panel loses strength and even the best hinges and fittings won't hold, leading to customer dissatisfaction and expensive replacements.

The TAPK Groove (Water-Drip Edge): Small Detail, Big Impact

An often-ignored feature in Indian kitchens is the **TAPK grooves** narrow channel milled into the underside of the stone near the front edge. This groove **breaks surface tension**, preventing water from running off the counter and onto cabinets or walls.

Think of it as a small rain guard for your kitchen counter, redirecting every drop before it becomes a problem.

Why the TAPK Groove Matters:

- Prevents water from traveling underneath the stone
- Reduces long-term moisture exposure to wall or base cabinets
- Adds virtually no cost (typically under ₹1000) yet drastically improves longevity

Despite its importance, **over 99% of modular kitchen installations skip this detail**, largely due to a lack of awareness among fabricators and installers.

Key Takeaways: Protecting Your Kitchen from Water Damage

- **Choose a top-mounted sink** for easier, more secure installation
- **Preserve and properly seal the stone collar**

- **Always include a TAPK groove,** it's a low-cost, high-impact feature

In modular kitchens, **every millimeter matters,** especially where water and stone meet. Taking care of these small yet crucial technical details ensure not just beauty, but functional durability that stands the test of time.

After all, the true test of design is not just how it looks on Day 1, but how it performs in Year 5.

> ***"Har drop ka raasta control karo, warna waqt ke saath sapne seep kar jaate hain."***

The Legacy We Leave

At **Universal Pride Interiors Pvt. Ltd.,** our journey spans over 14 years of learning, refining and delivering furniture solutions that don't just fill spaces but transform them into experiences. This book is a reflection of that journey built with knowledge, shaped by passion and driven by a vision of smarter, more sustainable living.

But this isn't the end; it's the beginning.

A beginning for **better design,** where form truly meets function.

A beginning for **responsible manufacturing**, where every choice respects people and the planet.

A beginning for the **next generation of modular thinking,** efficient, elegant and enduring.

Because legacies aren't built in a day, they're crafted over time, with intention, innovation and integrity.

Let's Build the Future Together!

Thank You for Giving This Book Your Valuable Time!

You've just explored what's almost like a Wikipedia of modular furniture and smarter interiors, a guide packed with real insights, practical comparisons and years of on-ground experience.

Now, you have two choices:

1. We have more than 40 critical points. To explore any of these in detail, please don't hesitate to contact us.

Or

2. If you'd like me to walk beside you or if this book sparked ideas or reaffirmed your belief in better systems and smarter spaces at any point, you can **schedule a 1-to-1 meeting** with me. For that, you can:

Drop me a mail: nitin.m@universalprideinteriors.com,

contact@universalprideinteriors.com

Call us: +91-9990013055, 7290038585

Visit us: www.universalprideinteriors.com

Modular furniture isn't just about saving space, it's about creating value. Let's create it together.

With Warm Regards,

Nitin Mehandia

#1 Sustainable Modular Furniture Blueprint